# HILLARY
## UNHINGED

*in her own words*

COMPILED BY THOMAS KUIPER

# HILLARY UNHINGED

Published by WND Books, Washington, D.C. WND Books is a registered trademark of WorldNetDaily.com, Inc. ("WND")

Book designed by Mark Karis

WND Books are available at special discounts for bulk purchases. WND Books also publishes books in electronic formats. For more information call (541) 474-1776 or visit www.wndbooks.com.

Paperback ISBN: 978-1-93806794-5
eBook ISBN: 978-1-938067-95-2

Library of Congress Cataloging-in-Publication Data Available

Printed in the United States of America
14 15 16 17 18 19 LSI 9 8 7 6 5 4 3 2 1

This book is full of nearly unbelievable words spoken by a veritable politician. In order to prove that we aren't making this up, use your smartphone to scan the square codes to see video clips of Hillary actually saying some of these outlandish quotes or articles that record her nonesense in perpetuity. To view all the videos in this book from your computer go to
YOUTUBE.COM/USER/THEWNDTV1

Download the **Scan** app on your smartphone for free. Then, open the app, point the camera at the code, and you're done! No need to take a photo or press a "scan" button.

*In order to use **Scan**, your device must have a built-in camera. When scanning codes that redirect to online content (such as websites), you will need Internet connectivity.

Download **Scan** on your smartphone today.

Available on the
App Store

ANDROID APP ON
Google play

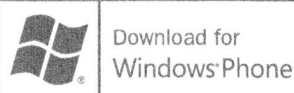
Download for
Windows Phone

# CONTENTS

"She's never forgotten where she came from.... From her mother's own childhood to going door-to-door... she's fought children and families all her career."

From Hillary's 2016 presidential bid announcement

# HELLO, HILLARY

"Part of what I believe with all my heart is that the voters are tired of people who lie to them. They're tired of people who act like something they're not."

In the famous January 26, 1992, interview with *60 Minutes*, Hillary's first major appearance before America, Hillary tried to assure the voters that the Clinton marriage was strong and that they could be trusted since they were telling the truth. (Newsbusters.org)

Liberal writer Carl Bernstein of Watergate fame writes of Hillary, "Since her Arkansas years, [she] always had a difficult relationship with the truth. . . . There is often a disconnect between her convictions and words, and her actions. This is where Hillary disappoints." (Bernstein, *A Woman In Charge*, 552, 554)

**ARTICLE**

"I'm not sittin' here like some little woman standin' by my man, like Tammy Wynette. I'm sittin' here because I love him, and I respect him, and I honor what he's been through, and what we've been through together, and if that's not enough for people, then heck, don't vote for him."

When Hillary found out that Tammy Wynette was furious about Hillary's comment in the 1992 *60 Minutes* interview, she stated, "I didn't mean to hurt Tammy Wynette as a person. I happen to be a country-western fan" (*Los Angeles Times*, 1992). Remember, too, that Hillary has "always been a Yankees fan."

VIDEO

VIDEO

"I don't understand why nothing's ever been said about a George Bush girlfriend . . . I understand he has a Jennifer too."

In the 1992 presidential campaign, Hillary attempted to spread rumors when she told journalist Gail Sheehy about President George H. W. Bush having a mistress to try to deflect attention away from Gennifer Flowers's allegations that she had an affair with Governor Bill Clinton. (*Vanity Fair*, 1992)

ARTICLE

## "The daughter of Willie Horton."

Hillary dismisses Gennifer Flowers's story as a right-wing conspiracy, after Ms. Flowers held a press conference in the early stages of the 1992 campaign to announce the relationship she had with then Governor Bill Clinton.

By invoking the name of Willie Horton, Hillary was attempting to blame Republicans for this scandal, just as she felt the Republicans were responsible for the Horton controversy in the 1988 presidential race against Michael Dukakis. Just one problem with Hillary's argument: it was Al Gore who first brought up Willie Horton against Dukakis in the 1988 Democratic primaries. (*Prime Time Live*, 1992)

"It was a personal decision, but it was prompted by political considerations."

The First Lady of Arkansas admits that her name change of Hillary Rodham to Hillary Clinton around 1982 was due, in part, to politics. (*Prime Time Live*, 1992)

VIDEO

# SAINT HILLARY

"I have to confess that it's crossed my mind that you could not be a Republican and a Christian from time to time."

First Lady Hillary's opinion about the opposition party. (*Washington Post*, 1997)

"I've always been a praying person."

Senator Clinton addressing a group of religious leaders shortly after the 2004 presidential election. A post-election analysis showed that George W. Bush scored well with religious voters (*The Boston Globe*, 2005). However, when it comes to Republicans who use their faith to help guide them in their political decisions, Hillary derisively says, "Some [Republicans] honestly feel they are motivated by the truth, they are motivated by a higher calling, they are motivated by, I guess, a direct line to the heavens." (*New York Times*, 2005)

ARTICLE

"No one can read the New Testament of our Bible without recognizing that Jesus had a lot more to say about how we treat the poor than most of the issues that were talked about in this election."

Senator Clinton lecturing America on how we should deal with the poor. (BostonHerald.com, 2004)

ARTICLE

# "Well good!"

How Mrs. Clinton responded when prior to the 1992 election a street person told her he was homeless. (Fox News, 2002)

**VIDEO**

"Ever since I was a little girl, I've tried to do what I thought was important and what I thought was right."

Hillary to Larry King while on her book tour for *Living History* (*Larry King Live*, 2003). Hillary's former minister, Rev. Donald Jones, writes of Hillary's faith, "She realizes absolutely the truth of the human condition, which is that you cannot depend on the basic nature of man to be good . . . You have to use power. And there is nothing wrong with wielding power in the pursuit of politics that will add to the human good. I think Hillary knows this. She is very much the sort of Christian who understands that the use of power to achieve social good is legitimate." (*New York Times Magazine*, 1993)

ARTICLE

"I admire people who try to be the same in public and in private, who try to be respectful of people, who listen to people, who don't discount others because of their points of view. And that's pretty much the model I've tried to follow."

Hillary's opined during a Booknotes interview in 1996. However, according to Secret Service agents, "When she's in front of the lights, she turns it on, and when the lights are off and she's away from the lights, she a totally different person. . . . She's very angry and sarcastic and is very hard on her staff. . . . She is a totally different person behind the scenes than what you see when she is being interviewed." (Kessler, *First Family Detail*, 22)

"I've always believed, and this goes back to their teachings and my church [Methodist] that because I was blessed enough to be healthy and have a strong, supportive family, I had an obligation to care for other people, to help them. It wasn't something you did as an afterthought, it was how you lived."

Hillary trying to justify big government. The Bible commands that Christians should take care of the poor. It does not command that their government should forcibly take money from one person and give it to another. (*Parade*, 1993)

"I want to be idealistic, I want to care for the world . . .
I hope you do as well."

First Lady Hillary Clinton urged Michigan University college
graduates on May 2, 1993, to follow her example and be as
idealistic as she is. A woman who worked on Hillary's senate
campaign said of her, "She's the most unbelievable actress I have
ever met. . . . She has this unbelievable ability to be a liar. She
is soulless." (Klein, *The Truth About Hillary*, 184–185)

**VIDEO**

"You know, there are ten commandments, not one. And one of them is, 'Thou shall not bear false witness against thy neighbor.' And I think when we get to talk about character, we need to look at the whole person. And we need to look at the kind of way that person conducts himself."

The First Lady of Arkansas in a clip from the *60 Minutes* interview from January 1992 that did not air (Newsbusters.org). "I've said before and I'll say again, if everybody in this country had the character that my wife has, we'd be a better place to live." (William Clinton, 1996)

"In the Bible it says they asked Jesus how many times you should forgive, and he said seventy times seven. Well, I want you all to know that I'm keeping a chart."

First Lady Hillary, speaking at the National Prayer Luncheon. (*The New Yorker*, 1994)

ARTICLE

"[I've always had] an obligation to care for other people, to help them. It wasn't something you did as an afterthought. It was how you lived."

Hillary expressed this sentiment to journalist Dotson Rader in a lengthy piece published in *Parade*, April 11, 1993. According to Liz Moynihan, wife of Senator Pat Moynihan, Hillary is duplicitous. "She would say or do anything that would forward her ambition. She can look you straight in the eye and lie, and sort of not know she's lying. Lying isn't a sufficient word; it's distortion—distorting the truth to fit the case." (Klein, *Truth About Hillary*, 169)

ARTICLE

"A budget is not just about numbers, projections and line items. A budget is really an embodiment of our values as a nation . . . it says something about what we, as a people, hold dear and believe is important. It is about who we are as Americans."

Senator Clinton criticizing President George W. Bush's budget in a April 5, 2001, press release.

"We're not about the money."

Hillary tells the American people in the 1992 campaign that she and Bill were just middle class, ordinary folks trying to do the right thing. Hillary also told people that she disdained the whole principle of making money through commodities speculation and condemned dealing in such large sums of money as not socially acceptable— such greed! It was later discovered she made over $100,000 trading in cattle futures. (Schweizer, *Do As I Say (Not As I Do)*, 96)

"Every decision we make about taxes is a decision about our values."

Hillary equates lower taxes with moral wrongdoing (Schweizer, *Do As I Say, (Not As I Do)*, 98). On their tax returns when Mr. Clinton was the Governor of Arkansas and his wife was a partner in a Little Rock law firm the Clintons had gone so far as to deduct $2 for a pair of Bill's used underwear donated to charities (*New York Times*, 1994)

ARTICLE

# HILLARY'S POTTY MOUTH

# "You stupid motherf**ker!"

First Lady Hillary to the newly sworn-in President Bill Clinton on inauguration day, January 20, 1993 (Brock, *The Seduction of Hillary Rodham*, 321). Brock, an ardent Hillary supporter, heads the left-wing media watchdog group Media Matters For America, which calls itself an organization "dedicated to comprehensively monitoring, analyzing, and correcting conservative misinformation in the U.S. media."

# "You f**king Jew Bastard!"

To Bill's campaign manager, Paul Fray, on the night Bill lost his election for the US House of Representatives in 1974 (Oppenheimer, *The State of A Union*, 153). This allegation of Hillary's temper came out in 2000, when she was running for the senate in New York. In August 2000, the *New York Post* arranged to have Mr. Fray take a polygraph examination to verify whether he was telling the truth about this incident. According to a state-licensed polygrapher, "There is no doubt in my mind that Mr. Fray is truthful." (*New York Post*, 2000)

"You ought to burn that goddamned thing . . ."

The First Lady of Arkansas, circa 1985, to her bodyguard L. D. Brown when he proudly displayed a picture of himself taken with First Lady Nancy Reagan (Brown, *Crossfire*, 69). Governor Bill Clinton later helped Brown get into the Central Intelligence Agency.

"Goddammit . . . You bastard . . .
It's your f\*\*king fault."

First Lady Hillary to President Clinton after receiving some
bad news about the Whitewater investigation, as overheard by
Robert "Buzz" Patterson (Patterson, *Dereliction of Duty*, 68).
From 1996 to 1998, Lieutenant Colonel Patterson was the
Senior Military Aide to President Bill Clinton. During that
time he was responsible for the President's Emergency Satchel,
also known as the "football," containing the launch codes for
nuclear weapons.

"That'll teach them to f**k with us."

Hillary to her aides after making her famous "vast right-wing conspiracy" statement on national television in the early days of the Lewinsky scandal (Noonan, *The Case Against Hillary Clinton*, 162). Former Clinton advisor Lanny Davis endorsed Hillary for president, writing, "She is one of the kindest, warmest, most empathetic and caring people in public life today . . . I know that in 2016 more and more people will come to know her as she truly is." (TheHill.com, 2014)

ARTICLE

"What the f\*\*k are you doing up there? You get back here right away."

The First Lady chastising President Clinton over the phone after she learned he floated a proposal for health care reform that differed from her plan of 100 percent coverage for all citizens (*The Survivor*, 188). Political commentator David Gergen, an advisor to four US Presidents, the last being Bill Clinton, wrote about his observations of the Clinton marriage: "A chipper president would arrive at the office in the morning, almost whistling as he whipped through papers. A phone would ring. It was a call from upstairs at the residence [Hillary] . . . as we started back to work, his mood would darken, his attention wander, and hot words would spew out. . . . What, I would wonder, had she said to him now?" (Gergen, *Eyewitness To Power*, 274)

**BOOK**

"I get really tough when people f\*\*k with me."

A joyful Senator Hillary Clinton upon hearing the news that she had won a surprising victory over Barack Obama in the New Hampshire primary, January 2008. (Heilemann and Halperin, *Game Change*, 190)

BOOK

"You sold out, you motherf**ker, you sold out!"

Circa 1970, Hillary Rodham, then a congressional staffer, yells at famous Democrat lawyer Joseph Califano, who was representing Coca-Cola executives testifying on Capitol Hill regarding child labor issues. (Califano, *Inside: A Public and Private Life*, 213)

"This is the kind of sh*t I have to put up with."

First Lady of Arkansas Hillary Clinton to friend Susan McDougal when given a pair of earrings in the shape of the logo for the Arkansas Razorbacks. (Stewart, *Blood Sport*, 105)

"The thing with Obama is that he can't be bothered, and there is no hand on the tiller half the time. . . . That's the story of the Obama presidency. No hand on the f**king tiller. . . . And you can't trust the motherf**ker."

The former Secretary of State opining to her friends about the Obama presidency circa May of 2013. (Klein, *Blood Feud: The Clintons vs. The Obamas*, xv)

BOOK

# "F**k her."

Circa 2007, Hillary's reaction when she found out her fellow Democrat Senator Claire McCaskill of Missouri publicly stated that Bill Clinton had been a "great leader, but I don't want my daughter near him" (*Game Change*, 51-52). Hillary then cancelled a planned fundraiser for McCaskill. Apparently Hillary had forgotten that she once said as First Lady, "I have a burning desire to do what I can, a desire to make the world around me . . . better for everybody." (Clinton and Osborne, *The Unique Voice of Hillary Clinton*, 70)

"If you want to remain on this detail, get your f**king ass over here and grab those bags."

First Lady Hillary to one of her Secret Service guards (Milton, *The First Partner*, 259). Liberal television pundit Chris Matthews said he personally witnessed Senator Clinton using a member of her Secret Service detail to carry her luggage while on a Washington to New York shuttle. Said Matthews, "[I saw] one large guy, rather embarrassed, rather sheepish, walking along with his own earphones carrying her bags. . . . Who in the senate gets a Sherpa to carry their bags for them? . . . I've never heard of a senator getting a bag carrier. Who pays for the airfare for this guy? Who pays for his lifestyle? Who pays his salary to walk around carrying her bags, so she can walk around light-handed, with nothing in her hands? . . . It looks like—you talk about Queen Elizabeth, this looks pretty regal." (*Hardball*, 2001)

## "F**k off."

At the height of the Lewisnsky scandal, First Lady Hillary's response to a uniformed Secret Service officer who greeted her with, 'Good morning, ma'am.' (Kessler, *First Family Detail*, 16)

"What the f**k did we come here for? There's no money here."

Hillary grew furious with her staff when they pulled up to a political rally at a farm in upstate New York and the event lacked big money donors. A member of the secret service assigned to guard Hillary during the 2000 senate race told Kessler that she "flew into rages when she thought her campaign staff had not corralled enough onlookers beforehand. Hillary had an explosive temper." (Kessler, *A Matter of Character*, 2–3)

# "She's a short, Irish bitch."

Hillary's opinion of *New York Times* columnist Maureen Dowd, who was a frequent Clinton critic. (*New York Post*, 2000)

It was Dowd who got Hollywood mogul David Geffen to go on the record about his disdain for the Clintons in the run up to the 2008 Democratic primaries and explain why he would be supporting Barack Obama. Said Geffen to Dowd, "Everybody in politics lies, but they do it with such ease, it's troubling." (*New York Times*, 2007)

ARTICLE

# SECRETARY OF STATE

"With all due respect, the fact is we had four dead Americans. Was it because of a protest? Or was it because of guys out for a walk one night who decided they would go kill some Americans? What difference at this point does it make?"

Secretary of State Hillary Clinton's famous answer to questions about the Benghazi attack. (Senate Hearing 216, 2013)

VIDEO

"Those who exploit this tragedy over and over as a political tool minimize the sacrifice of those who served our country. I will not be a part of a political slugfest on the backs of dead Americans. It's just plain wrong, and it's unworthy of our great country. Those who insist on politicizing the tragedy will have to do so without me."

The former Secretary of State takes the high road when it comes to the Benghazi controversy (Clinton, *Hard Choices*, 414).

**ARTICLE**

"The president knew what? My constituents would like to know the answer to that and many other questions, not to blame the president or any other American, just to know."

When she received criticism for making what many thought to be an irresponsible, partisan attack, she responded, "We have a responsibility to ask for information, and I think that is not only appropriate but necessary." However, years earlier then-Senator Hillary Clinton criticized President George W. Bush implying he had advance knowledge of the 9/11 attacks and did nothing to stop them.

### ARTICLE

In 2009 Secretary of State Hillary Clinton learned a valuable lesson when she presented Russian Foreign Minister Sergei Lavrov with a gift bearing an incorrect translation. Clinton presented Lavrov with a gift-wrapped red button which said "Reset" in English and *Peregruzka* in Russian.

**"We worked hard to get the right Russian word. Do you think we got it right?"** Clinton asked Lavrov.

"You got it wrong, this says 'peregruzka' which means overcharged," said Lavrov.

Clinton said she was presenting the button because **"it represents what President Obama and Vice President Biden and I have been saying, and that is, 'We want to reset our relationship.' And so we will do it together."**

ARTICLE

ARTICLE

In spite of the deteriorating relations between Russia and the United States since Obama took office, in July 2014 Hillary actually stated, **"The reset worked."**

"Great nations need organizing principles, and 'Don't do stupid stuff' is not an organizing principle."

The former Secretary of State criticizes Obama's foreign policy (*The Atlantic*, 2014). Is a cheap, plastic red button an organizing principle?

ARTICLE

"Obama has turned into a joke. . . . [He's] allowed his hatred for his enemies to screw him the way Nixon did."

May 2013 Hillary gave her opinion of her former boss (Klein, *Blood Feud: The Clintons vs. The Obamas*, xiv). It got back to the Obamas that Bill Clinton, in trying to obtain Ted Kennedy's endorsement for Hillary in the 2008 primaries, made a racist statement about Obama. Recounting the conversation later to a friend, Kennedy fumed that had Bill Clinton told him that a few years ago, this guy would have been getting us coffee. (Heilemann and Halperin, *Game Change*, 218)

# HILLARY ON MONEY

"You have no reason to remember, but we came out of the White House not only dead broke, but in debt. We had no money when we got there, and we struggled to piece together the resources for mortgages for houses, for Chelsea's education. It was not easy."

Hillary's famous "Dead Broke" comment, trying to explain how tough it was for them when they left the White House in January 2001 (ABC News, 2014). Hillary received an $8 million book advance and Bill a $12 million advance on his memoirs as they were leaving the White House. In December 2000 they bought a seven-bedroom house near Embassy Row in Washington, DC. The price was $2.85 million. The *New York Times* reported that the Clintons put $855,000 down on the Washington house.

**VIDEO**

"The last time I actually drove a car myself was 1996."

Hillary Clinton in a speech to the National Automobile Dealers Association in New Orleans. One of the issues Hillary Clinton plans to take up in the 2016 election is wealth inequality, which may be hard to do if you've been driven around in a limo for the last twenty years. Per the *Washington Post*, she charges a $300k fee to speak at college campuses. When UCLA wanted to have her speak at their college and found out her fee was $300,000, they asked for a discounted rate as they were a public university. They were told $300,000 is the "special university rate." (*Washington Post*, 2014)

**VIDEO**

"Don't let anybody tell you that it's corporations and businesses that create jobs. You know that old theory, trickle-down economics. That has been tried; that has failed. It has failed rather spectacularly."

Hillary Clinton at a campaign rally for Senate candidate Martha Coakley on October 25, 2014. That gaff caused Hillary to go into serious CYA mode, issuing subsequent statements "clarifying" her remarks. "Trickle down economics has failed. I short-handed this point the other day, so let me be absolutely clear about what I've been saying for a couple of decades. Our economy grows when businesses and entrepreneurs create good-paying jobs." (*New York Magazine*, 2014)

VIDEO

"The rich are not paying their fair share in any nation that is facing the kind of employment issues [like the US]."

Perhaps too many rich people are deducting $2.00 for every pair of used underwear they donate to charities? (*Fox News*, 2010)

VIDEO

"Too many people have made too much money off of eliminating opportunities for caring for people instead of expanding those."

First Lady Hillary Clinton on trying to justify a government takeover of healthcare, something she couldn't accomplish but her nemesis has nearly done. (*Chicago Tribune*, 1993).

# "It takes a village to raise a child."

One of Hillary Clinton's favorite quotes, and one she paraphrased to use as a title to her book on child-rearing, *It Takes A Village,* which came out in 1996.

Apparently, it takes a village to tip a waitress. When running for the senate in 2000, First Lady Hillary Clinton was treated to a free breakfast for herself and her entourage. At the end of the meal, they all left without tipping the waitress. The waitress, a single mother who made $2.90 per hour plus tips also did not have any health insurance. At first, Mrs. Clinton denied the charge, "That's just another wild story." After realizing the story was true, Hillary then called the waitress, "She apologized for not giving a tip. . . . She said I was a sweetheart." But she didn't say anything about a forthcoming tip. "She didn't offer, and I didn't ask," said the waitress stiffed by Hillary (*Washington Times*, 2000). It was reported that Mrs. Clinton later sent the waitress a $100 savings bond for her son.

### ARTICLE

"They don't see me as part of the problem . . . because we pay ordinary income tax, unlike a lot of people who are truly well off, not to name names, and we've done it through the dint of hard work."

Hillary Clinton on whether she and her husband's wealth may hurt her chances to connect with Democrats in the next election (*Guardian*, 2014). The Clintons net worth is reported to be over $100 million dollars, gained through the hard work of flying on private jets to give speeches at $300,000 each.

ARTICLE

# REVISIONIST HILLARY HISTORY

"And for a long time after, I would wake up in the middle of the night worrying that the actions and reactions concerning the travel office helped drive Vince Foster to take his own life. . . . I wondered ceaselessly whether this tragedy could have been prevented if I or anyone had noticed something amiss in Vince's behavior."

Hillary ruminated over the Whitewater scandal in her book *Living History* (page 173 and 176). According to FBI agents investigating Whitewater, what never came out publicly was that the agents learned about a week before Foster's suicide he and Hillary were part of a meeting with other White House aides to go over the health care legislation she was proposing. When Foster raised a legal objection at this meeting, Hillary "violently disagreed" and "put him down really, really bad in a pretty good-size meeting," according to several witnesses. An FBI agent reported that Hillary "told him [Foster] that if he didn't get the picture, he would always be a little hick-town lawyer who was obviously not ready for the big-time." He also stated, "The put-down that she gave him in that big meeting just pushed him over the edge. . . . It was the straw that broke the camel's back." (Kessler, *The Secrets of the FBI*, 108–09)

"I respect and admire the [Secret Service] agents I've met over the years. . . . My family and I have also come to know the agents as warm, funny and thoughtful human beings."

Hillary recounted in her book *Living History* (page 451). According to Ronald Kessler, "She is so nasty to agents that being assigned to her detail is considered a form of punishment. It shines a light on her character," Kessler said. "She claims to be a champion of the little people, and she's going to help the middle class. And, in fact, she treats these people around her, [who] would lay down their lives for her, like sub-humans; and I think voters need to consider that." (Kessler, *First Family Detail*)

**VIDEO**

"I made my share of mistakes. And mistakes in New York politics aren't easily brushed aside. When the Yankees came to the White House to celebrate their World Series win in 1999, manager Joe Torre gave me a cap, which I promptly donned. Bad move."

Hillary tells this tale in her book *Living History* (page 509). Chris Matthews had some fun at Hillary's expense when she first ran for the Senate, saying "She tried hard to prove she was a Noo Yawker." He ran a clip of the 1999 interview with Katie Couric where she stated, "I've always been a Yankees fan." After showing the clip, Matthews said: "I just love the way Katie Couric went at her there: 'Come on, how many hats you wearing, babe?' I just think that was great." (*Chris Matthews Show*, 2007)

**VIDEO**

"As with many of the good and bad things that have been said about me over the years, reports of my 'legendary temper' are exaggerated."

Hillary's world from her eyes and as she explained in her book *Living History* (page 166). According to former Clinton aide Jake Siewert, "She was the only person in the White House that people were afraid of." (Harris, *The Survivor*, 97)

"The [Secret] Service uses code names for its protectees, and each member of a family has a name beginning with the same letter. Bill became 'Eagle,' I was 'Evergreen' . . . The code names sound whimsical, but they mask a harsh reality: Ongoing threats require the vigilance and intrusiveness of protective security."

This is more insight from Hillary from her book *Living History* (page 137). Interestingly, Bill Clinton had a buxom, blond mistress who visited so often when Hillary wasn't home that the former president's Secret Service detail gave her an unofficial code name: Energizer. (Kessler, *The First Family Detail*, 2)

"Bill and I were increasingly disturbed by the fervor with which the GOP leaders spouted rhetoric that attacked government."

First Lady Hillary Clinton was upset that Republicans were criticizing the Clinton administration. *Living History* (page 291). However, when it was her turn to attack the government when she was a senator and George W. Bush was president, she shouted . . .

"I am sick and tired of people who say that if you debate and you disagree with this administration, somehow you're not patriotic, and we should stand up and say, 'We are Americans and we have a right to debate and disagree with any administration!'"

VIDEO

"Ted Kennedy . . . is one of the most effective Senators who has ever served our country and is also an expert sailor."

An expert sailor? Really? Senator Edward Kennedy famously endorsed Obama over Hillary in the 2008 Democratic primaries. What was not commonly known was how much Mrs. Clinton rubbed the Kennedys the wrong way from the start. Kennedy held the view "that the Clintons were entitled climbers . . . and was known to roll his eyes" at Hillary when she spoke on various topics that he had spent years working on in the Senate prior to her getting there. (Halper, *Clinton, Inc.*, 42)

"As Chief of Staff, [Leon Panetta] ran a tight ship. . . . His expertise in Congress and with the budget would prove to be of crucial importance in the budget battle ahead."

Hillary correctly praising one of her husband's best appointments in *Living History*. Panetta, however, never was comfortable with the Clintons. "He was troubled, he told friends, by the anger and insecurity the Clintons showed in private moments. The couple might be chatting away . . . when suddenly the conversation would pivot to an angry discussion of some old political enemy from Arkansas. It almost seemed a touch paranoid to Panetta." (Harris, *The Survivor*, 218)

"My husband may have his faults, but he has never lied to me."

Hillary recounts a conversation she had with an advisor just prior to Bill's confession of his affair with Monica Lewinsky. Bill Clinton allegedly told Monica Lewinsky that he'd had hundreds of affairs (*Living History*, 465).

"[Paula Jones] said she wanted to clear her name. But instead of announcing a libel suit against the *[American] Spectator*, she accused Bill Clinton of sexually harassing her by making unwanted advances. . . . We expected this story to die like the other phony scandals."

Hillary wrote this in *Living History* (page 227), but upon further review, the scandal was not so phony after all, as it led to her husband's impeachment. Also, in 2005 Paula Jones passed a polygraph examination regarding whether Bill Clinton sexually harassed her.

"My husband has one of the most extraordinary strengths of character of anyone I have ever met or even read about."

Hillary told Parade magazine in 1993. Bill Clinton's character is so strong that after allegedly raping Juanita Broaddrick and biting her lip, he put on his sunglasses and advised her, "You better put some ice on that" as he left the room. (*Wall Street Journal*, 1999)

"By then Bill's entire life was under a media microscope. . . . While the mainstream press still avoided printing unsubstantiated rumors, the supermarket tabloids were offering cash for shocking stories from Arkansas. Eventually one of these fishing expeditions hooked a whale of a tale."

Another whale of a tale from *Living History* (page 106) that upon further review turned out to be true, since Bill Clinton admitted to having an affair with Gennifer Flowers.

"The great story here for anybody willing to find it and write about it and explain it is this vast right-wing conspiracy that has been conspiring against my husband since the day he announced for president."

Hillary's famous denial about the allegations of her husband having a relationship with White House intern Monica Lewinsky (*Today*, 1998). Upon further review, the allegations were true. However, Hillary still blames the vast right-wing conspiracy.

**VIDEO**

"You know, when I made the comment about the vast right-wing conspiracy, I wasn't kidding. What I never could've predicted is that it was not a conspiracy—it was wide open and out there for everybody to see."

VIDEO

"It had two *L*s, which is how she thought she was supposed to spell Hillary. So when I was born, she called me Hillary, and she always told me it's because of Sir Edmund Hillary."

First Lady Hillary Clinton explaining how she got her name, upon meeting Sir Edmund Hillary in 1995 (*New York Times*, 1995).

Upon further review, in 2006 Hillary's staff admitted she wasn't named after the famous mountain climber after all, as Sir Edmund became famous only after climbing Everest in 1953. Hillary Rodham was born in 1947 (*New York Times*, 2006).

**ARTICLE**

"I had no role in the decision to terminate the [travel office] employees."

First Lady Hillary denying any involvement in the fiasco that came to be known as Travelgate (*Newsweek*, 1996). Upon further review, it was Hillary's doing. Robert Ray, the Independent Counsel who took over from Ken Starr, wrote that "Mrs. Clinton's sworn testimony that she had no input into . . . the Travel Office firings is factually inaccurate. . . . Mrs. Clinton's input into process was significant, if not the significant factor influencing the pace of events in the Travel Office firings and the ultimate decision to fire the employees." (ABCNews.com, 2000)

# HILLARY VS. BARACK

"I'm in. And I'm in to win."

Senator Clinton announcing her intention to run for the presidency, on January 20, 2007, via her website. She lost.

"So let's talk. Let's chat. Let's start a dialogue about your ideas and mine."

More from Hillary's announcement to run for the presidency, January 2007.

According to President Clinton's first press secretary, Dee Dee Myers, Hillary was not always open to the ideas of others. She once viciously attacked George Stephanopoulos when he tried to have a dialogue about how to handle the growing Whitewater controversy. "She just jumped down my throat . . . it was fierce and chilling," said Stephanopoulos. (Harris, *The Survivor*, 116)

"So, I'm in it for the long run. It's not a very long run. It will be over by February 5th."

Speaking to journalist George Stephanopoulos, a former staff member of the Clintons, Hillary was expecting to wrap up the nomination in just a month's time (*This Week*, 2007). The primary race lasted until June of 2008, when she lost.

ARTICLE

"[It was] a great experience in every respect."

This was Hillary's response in 2004 when asked about her experience as a board member of Walmart (*AP*, 2006). In the 2008 Democratic primary battle, Senator Obama said to Hillary, "While I was working on those streets, watching those folks see their jobs shipped overseas, you were a corporate lawyer sitting on the board of Walmart!"

"As a shareholder and director of our company, I'm always proud of Walmart and what we do and the way we do it better than anybody else."

Hillary praised the antiunion company in the 1980s when she served on its board.

VIDEO

"Great victory, we're three tickets out of Iowa, see you in New Hampshire."

Hillary's only words when she called Barack Obama to congratulate him on winning the Iowa Caucuses in 2008. Some of her advisors who heard this call "found the display they were witnessing now utterly stunning—and especially unnerving coming from Hillary. Watching her bitter and befuddled reaction, her staggering lack of calm or command, one of her senior-most lieutenants thought for the first time, 'This woman shouldn't be president.'" (Heilemann and Halperin, *Game Change*, 6)

## "Why do they hate me so much?"

Hillary asking members of her staff when her attempt to be nice with her traveling press was met with stony silence (Heilemann and Halperin, *Game Change*,172). Could it be due to the fact the press had dealt with her spokesperson, Philippe Reines? In one famous exchange with a reporter of an online news website, Reines called the reporter "an unmitigated asshole," then taunted him by asking, "How's that for a non-bullsh*t response? Now that we've gotten that out of our systems, have a good day. And by good day, I mean F*** Off." (*BuzzFeed*, 2012)

"I've had people say, 'I wish I could vote for both of you.' Well, that might be a possibility someday."

Hillary Clinton suggesting that Barack Obama would make a fine choice to be her vice-president in the 2008 election. The only problem was, at the time she stated this, Obama had won more of the popular vote and won more delegates than Clinton. Said an astonished Obama, "I don't know how somebody who's in second place can offer the vice presidency to someone who's in first place." (*New York Times*, 2008)

"I have a much broader base to build a winning coalition on. . . . Obama's support on working, hard working Americans, white Americans, is weakening again, and how whites in both states who had not completed college were supporting me."

Clinton said in an interview with *USA Today* in 2008.

"America needs a president that will stand up for them, not a president that looks down on them."

Hillary's comments after Obama said people in small-town Middle America bitterly cling to their guns and religion (Heilemann and Halperin, *Game Change*, 241).

"I suppose I could have stayed home and baked cookies and had teas, but what I decided to do was to fulfill my profession."

Hillary's famous gaff from the 1992 campaign.

ARTICLE

# "Shame on you, Barack Obama!"

Hillary fuming at her opponent in the 2008 primary battle because he had the gall to point out she had changed her position on supporting NAFTA, an agreement her husband signed while president.

**VIDEO**

"I'm sorry, but he was such an asshole."

Senator Clinton's opinion of Barack Obama after a nasty primary debate in the 2008 primary contest (Heilemann and Halperin, *Game Change*, 206).

"I don't get it. Can you tell me what it is about this guy?"


A frustrated Hillary asking her friend why Obama was connecting so well with the voters. This caused her friend to state, "With all due respect, ma'am, a lot of it is that he's not you." (Halper, *Clinton, Inc.*, 120)

"It's not us making this charge, it's the media."

Hillary denying her campaign is accusing Senator Obama of plagiarism (Politico, 2008).

(Two days later)

"Lifting whole passages from someone else's speeches is not change you can believe in. Its change you can Xerox."

Hillary charging Obama with plagiarism at a presidential debate (AP, 2008).

VIDEO

"Who does he think he is? Drives me nuts. Drives me nuts! He has no sense of history at all!"

Hillary upset with Obama in the 2008 primaries, when he made a positive comment about the ideas of the Reagan Revolution (Heilemann and Halperin, *Game Change*, 200).

## "I helped to bring peace to Northern Ireland"

Hillary told CNN's American Morning in 2008. David Trimble, the leader of the Ulster Unionist Party in Northern Ireland who shared a Nobel Peace Prize for the settlement said Clinton's claim was "a wee bit silly." He didn't want to rain on "the thing for her, but being a cheerleader for something is slightly different from being a principal player." (*Daily Telegraph*, 2008)

"[Obama] was a part-time state senator for a few years, and then he came to the Senate and immediately started running for president."

Hillary's opinion of her democratic rival in the early days of the 2008 primary battle (*USA Today*, 2008).

"[Senator McCain has] never been the president, but he will put forth his lifetime of experience. I will put forth my lifetime of experience. Senator Obama will put forth a speech he made in 2002."

Hillary on Obama's thin resume in the 2008 primaries (CBS News, 2008).

ARTICLE

"Just imagine, just for fun, if my pastor from Arkansas said the kind of things his pastor said . . . I'm just saying. Just imagine. This race would be over."

Hillary's reaction upon hearing many of the controversial things from Obama's pastor and calling out the mainstream media for covering up for candidate Obama (Heilemann and Halperin, *Game Change*, 239).

"My husband did not wrap up the nomination in 1992 until he won the California primary somewhere in the middle of June, right? We all remember Bobby Kennedy was assassinated in June in California. You know, I just, I don't understand it."

When Clinton gave this explanation for not dropping out of the 2008 Democrat primary, Keith Olbermann ranted "This, Senator, is too much! Because a senator, a politician, a person, who can let hang in mid-air, the prospect that she just might be sticking around, in part, just in case the other guy gets shot, has no business being, and no capacity to be, the President of the United States!" (MSNBC, 2008)

VIDEO

"I've already done that job."

After Obama won the primary and Hillary conceded defeat, many of her supporters were insisting that Obama offer her the vice-presidency. She dismissed it, using this reason (Heilemann and Halperin, *Game Change*, 261).

"I think she was a disaster . . . She turned out not to be able to manage . . . She didn't even know which trains she was supposed to schedule . . . And I feel terrible, because it wasn't a campaign worthy of me."

Hillary's opinion of her long-time aide, Patty Solis Doyle, who was her campaign manager from the 2008 primaries (Heilemann and Halperin, *Game Change*, 266).

"Unity is not only a beautiful place, it's a wonderful feeling, isn't it? I know what we start here in this field of unity will end on the steps of the Capitol when Barack Obama takes the oath of office."

A joint appearance by Hillary Clinton and Barack Obama in Unity, New Hampshire, expressing their unity after a contentious primary battle in 2008. (New York Times, 2008)

Bill Clinton was so inspired by this show of unity in Unity that he made a trip to Intercourse, Pennsylvania.

"He took a lie detector test. I had him take a polygraph, which he passed, which forever destroyed my faith in polygraphs."

A younger Hillary Clinton can be heard on audio laughing as she discusses defending a child-rapist back in 1975. The rape victim recently stated that when Hillary defended the rapist and attacked her (the victim), she (Hillary) "took me through hell."(Daily Beast, 2014)

VIDEO

# DODGING SNIPER FIRE

"Due to reports of snipers in the hills around the airstrip, we were forced to cut short an event on the tarmac with local children, though we did have time to meet them and their teachers. . . . One eight-year-old girl gave me a copy of a poem she had written entitled 'Peace.'")

Hillary describing her trip to Bosnia in 1996 in her book *Living History* (page 343), which came out in 2004.

**VIDEO**

"We used to say in the White House that if a place is too dangerous, too small, or too poor, send the First Lady."

By December of 2007 Hillary embellished the story on the campaign trail. (*Meet The Press*, 2008). In this speech she was leaving out the fact that she brought along her daughter, singer Sheryl Crow, and the comedian Sinbad.

**VIDEO**

"We landed in one of those corkscrew landings and ran out because they said there might be sniper fire. I don't remember anyone offering me tea on the tarmac when that was happening."

Another statement on December 29, 2007; she was perhaps referring to her famous "cookies and teas" comment from the 1992 campaign (*Meet The Press*, 2008).

"I remember, particularly, a trip to Bosnia, where the welcoming ceremony had to be moved inside because of sniper fire."

By the end of February 2008, the story had changed. (*Meet The Press*, 2008).

By St. Patrick's Day, March 17, 2008, she stated:

"I remember landing under sniper fire. There was supposed to be some kind of a greeting ceremony at the airport, but instead we just ran with our heads down to get into the vehicles, to get to our base."

(*Meet The Press*, 2008)

**VIDEO**

"There was no greeting ceremony, and we basically were told to run to our cars. Now that is what happened."

"I was told we had to land a certain way, we had to have our bullet proof stuff on because of the threat of sniper fire. I was also told the greeting ceremony had been moved away from the tarmac. But there was this 8 year old girl, and I said, "I can't rush by her, I've got to at least greet her.' So I greeted her, I took her stuff, and I left. Now that's my memory of it."

In an interview with the Philadelphia Daily News, on March 20, 2008, Hillary still could not accurately state what had happened. (Philly.com, 2008)

"I was sleep deprived, and I misspoke."


Hillary attempting to explain her sniper fire fib (CBS News, 2008). However, during this same period Hillary argued that she was more qualified to be president than Obama to take a 3:00 AM phone call.

# THE VAST CONSPIRACIES

## "[They] set Bill up."

Hillary opining that Michael Dukakis and his advisors sabotaged Bill Clinton when he gave the introduction speech for Dukakis at the 1988 Democratic Convention. (Hubbell, *Friends In High Places: Our Journey from Little Rock to Washington, DC*, 144). The "introduction" speech dragged on for thirty minutes and was a major embarrassment for then-Governor Clinton.

"[The Secret Service] will shut down the entire Eastern Seaboard just to embarrass us if we give them the excuse . . . They're mainly Republicans. They hate us. They always take the most extreme option just to cause us embarrassment."

First Lady Hillary's opinion of the US Secret Service to advisor Dick Morris (Morris, *Rewriting History*, 137).

"Do you know why these reporters keep attacking us? Keep investigating us? Because they're jealous . . . and they can't get over the fact that we're here [in the White House] and they're not."

First Lady Hillary to Dick Morris after being criticized by the press (Morris, *Rewriting History*, 60)

"The media misunderstand me. I am actually very traditional in most of my beliefs, especially social issues."

First Lady Hillary to presidential advisor David Gergen, blaming the press for the image that she was pulling President Clinton too far to the left (Gergen, *Eyewitness To Power*, 267–68).

"I'm not going to have some reporters pawing through our papers. We are the president."

First Lady Hillary Clinton, who was co-president—in her opinion (Stewart, *Blood Sport*, 368). She would later solve this problem of people pawing through her papers by setting up her own e-mail account on her own server while she was secretary of state.

"I mean, you've got a conservative and/or right-wing press presence with really nothing on the other end of the political spectrum, so that most of what is left in what you might call the middle or the establishment or the mainstream tries to be objective and tries to be thoughtful."

In 2007 Clinton admitted to helping to start Media Matters and the Center For American Progress.

**VIDEO**

"If all that were proven true, that would be a very serious offense. This is not going to be proven true."

A statement by Hillary in the early days of the Lewinsky scandal regarding the vast right-wing conspiracy. Of course, the charges were proven true and her husband admitted it.

VIDEO

"That was a very painful time for me, for my family, and for our country. . . . Obviously, I didn't mislead anyone. I didn't know the truth, and there's a great deal of pain associated with that."

In a September 2000 senate debate with Rick Lazio this was Hillary's response to Russert's question about whether or not she regretted misleading the American people in the Monica Lewinsky scandal?

Hamilton Jordan, who was chief of staff for President Jimmy Carter, writes of her "pain," "Instead of leaving [Bill] for his public betrayal, Hillary Clinton exploited her public image of a wronged but loyal spouse to create a new persona for herself and win election to the senate" *Wall Street Journal*, 2001).

VIDEO

ARTICLE

# THE SMARTEST WOMAN IN THE WORLD?

"I ended up voting for the resolution after carefully reviewing the information and the intelligence that I had available."

Senator Clinton explaining to members of the liberal group Code Pink why she voted for the Iraq war (*New York Magazine*, 2007). In the 2008 primaries, Hillary was forced to admit she did not read the NIE—National Intelligence Estimate—which was the case for going to war. She, instead, had to concede that she had been "briefed" on it. (*ABC News*, 2015)

"This is what we call smart power, using every possible tool and partner to advance peace and security, leaving no one on the sidelines. Showing respect, even for one's enemies. Trying to understand and in so far as psychologically possible, empathize with their perspective and point of view."

Hillary at Georgetown University suggesting America be more flexible and understanding of our enemies (*ABC News*, 2014). This gaff by Hillary caused political commentator George Will to say, "Let me try to say this as politely as possible—the English language is not Hillary Clinton's close friend."

**VIDEO**

"I knew nothing about my brother's involvement in these pardons. I knew nothing about his taking money for his involvement. I had no knowledge of that whatsoever."

Hillary is utilizing Sgt. Schultz defense when she comments about the pardon scandals. Her husband issued many controversial pardons in the final days of his administration and her brother was paid over $200,000 for obtaining one for a convicted drug runner. (*Crossfire*, 2001)

"We could make that one of the biggest tourist attractions in the country. I love baseball—but there are more women than baseball players."

Senator Clinton wanted federal funds for a National Women's Hall of Fame, which she thought could outdraw the Baseball Hall of Fame in Cooperstown. (AP Blog, 2006)

"I don't believe [children] are ready for sex or its potential consequences . . . and I think we need to do everything in our power to discourage sexual activity and encourage abstinence."

Clinton's take on raising children as portrayed in *It Takes A Village* (page 161). Does this apply to presidents and White House interns?

"Millions of children in America are carrying around something that could kill them someday. I'm not talking about guns or drugs. I'm talking about excess weight."

Senator Clinton wrote these words just three days after the London bombings by Arab youths. (*Post Star*, 2005)

"I don't talk about my personal business, and I feel strongly that what goes on in a marriage or a family should remain in that marriage and in that family."

After the Clinton's marriage "survived" the Lewinsky scandal she seemed to want to keep her private life under wraps when asked about her troubled marriage by Larry King in 2000 (*Larry King Live*, 2000). However, for the price of just $8,000,000, Hillary was willing to open up about that time in her marriage in her memoir. "I could hardly breathe. Gulping for air, I started crying and yelling at him . . . Why did you lie to me?"(Clinton, *Living History*, 466)

"I didn't have the benefit of a Democratic Congress."

Senator Clinton's excuse for failing to deliver on her campaign promise to create 200,000 new jobs in upstate New York (*Syracuse Post-Standard,* 2006).

"I wanted desperately to be an Olympic athlete. I tried everything. . . . I couldn't jump, I couldn't run, I couldn't swim. . . . So I wrote to NASA and said, 'How do I sign up to be an astronaut?' And they wrote back very politely and said, 'We don't take girls.'"

Senator Clinton explaining that she was not talented to do anything else, so she chose politics (*Newsday*, 2006). The first woman astronaut, Sally Ride, is almost the same age as Hillary, so her story about NASA not taking girls has little credibility.

"Within and beyond their homes, adults must speak out against racial, ethnic, religious, or gender slurs."

Hillary explained in her 1996 book, *It Takes a Village* (page 188). When asked if she's ever used an ethnic slur, Hillary stated, "I've never done it; I've never thought it." In 2004, Senator Clinton joked that Mahatma Gandhi "ran a gas station in St. Louis." She was forced to apologize, calling it "a lame attempt at humor."

"All women who care about equality of opportunity, about integrity, and morality in the workplace are in Professor Hill's debt."

In a 1992 speech before the American Bar Association, Hillary Clinton praised Anita Hill, the woman who accused Supreme Court nominee Clarence Thomas of sexual harassment (Brock, *The Real Anita Hill*, 12).She also said at this function, "As women and as lawyers, we must never again shy from raising our voices against sexual harassment." Kathleen Willey is still waiting to hear if Hillary will speak out against her husband's harassment of women.

"We just can't trust the American people to make those types of choices . . . Government has to make those choices for people."

First Lady Hillary Clinton speaking to Rep. Dennis Hastert, R-IL, on whether citizens get to have a say in how to spend their money in her health care reform plan (Brock, *The Seduction of Hillary Rodham*, 334). Hastert wrote of this meeting with Hillary in his autobiography, "As Hillary Clinton once told me . . . people are basically greedy and won't make the tough decisions. They won't take their kid to the hospital when he needs to go because they want to keep the money for themselves." (Hastert, *Speaker*, 249)

"We're all going to have to rethink how we deal with the internet. As exciting as these new developments are, there are a number of serious issues without any kind of editing function or gatekeeping function."

Just a few weeks after the Monica Lewinsky scandal was reported by the Drudge Report, Hillary made a speech about this disturbing new trend of free speech and freedom of the press on the Internet (SFGate.com, 1998).

ARTICLE

"Many of you are well enough off that [President George W. Bush's] tax cuts may have helped you. We're saying that for America to get back on track, we're probably going to cut that short and not give it to you. We're going to take things away from you on behalf of the common good."

Senator Clinton's remarks in a speech in San Francisco to many of her fellow wealthy liberals (SFGate.com, 2004).

"I am, you know, adamantly against illegal immigrants."

Senator Clinton quoted in February 2003 (*Washington Times*, 2004)

"We should not unduly punish the overwhelming majority of immigrants who work hard, raise families, pay their taxes, and contribute to their communities."

"People need to stop employing illegal immigrants."

She then criticized Republicans for introducing legislation which attempted to curb illegal immigration, "It is certainly not in keeping with my understanding of the scriptures, because this bill would literally criminalize the Good Samaritan, and probably even Jesus himself." (Buchanan, *Extreme Makeover of Hillary (Rodham) Clinton.*)

"We should all remember . . . that this is about peoples' lives. This is about, I would venture to guess, the people who served us tonight, who prepared our food tonight . . . These are the lives of people who are, in many instances, longtime residents and workers who have not only raised children, but made contributions."

Hillary supporting President Obama's executive order on immigration (MSNBC.com, 2014). The hotel where Hillary made these comments later issued a statement saying they do not employ illegal aliens.

"There's so much anger in large parts of the electorate right now, people whose incomes have not rebounded from the Great Recession . . . Where people feel . . . they are not being viewed as important to employers, to their government, in the community . . . They feel that something is not working."

Former Secretary of State Hillary Clinton commenting on voter frustration (MSNBC, 2014). Hillary conveniently omitted the fact that she and the Democrats had been in charge the previous six years.

"On this Lord's Day, let us say with one voice, the words of James Cleveland's great freedom hymn: [at this point she adopts a southern accent] 'I don't feel no ways tired. I come too far from where I started from. Nobody told me that the road would be easy. I don't believe he brought me this far, to leave me.'"

Hillary speaking at First Baptist Church in Selma, Alabama on March 4, 2007. She later explained her southern accent to a group of black journalists by saying, "I lived all those years in Arkansas, and you know, I'm in this inter-racial marriage." (Bill Clinton has been called "America's first black president.")

**VIDEO**

"If there's one thing I've learned over the last seven years, it's how to hold my tongue."

First Lady Hillary Clinton in the final years of her husband's presidency. If only this were true. (Sheehy, *Hillary's Choice*, 363)

# HOLD YOUR TONGUE

"On January 20, 1994, the administration's one-year anniversary, Janet Reno announced the appointment of Robert Fiske as special prosecutor . . . If he had been left to do his job, my concerns . . . would have proved unfounded."

Hillary explained in *Living History* (page 219). When asked about claims that there was "nothing" to the Whitewater investigation, Robert Fiske, the first special prosecutor, had this to say: "There were indictments, there were convictions . . . People went to jail. There was never any evidence that was sufficient to link the Clintons to any of it, but there were certainly serious crimes." (Yahoo News, 2014)

"I feel very confident about how this will all turn out. This is not a long-term problem or issue in any way."

First Lady Hillary Clinton during a press conference explaining away the growing Whitewater scandal.

**VIDEO**

"Shoulda, woulda, coulda, we didn't."

During a press conference about Whitewater, Hillary dismissed a reporter's question about whether the Clintons should have been more aware of potential wrongdoing and the appearance of impropriety (Woodward, *Shadow*, 253). When a bank officer tried to warn Hillary that the legal document she was drafting in the Whitewater deal was an illegal transaction, she dismissed his concern by saying, in effect, that he was to worry about getting the deal done, and she would worry about the law (*Frontline: Once Upon A Time In Arkansas*, 1997).

"Well, you know, I, that was a long time ago, I have to remember . . ."

Senator Clinton stammering an answer when asked if Walmart still had the same employment practices as when she was on their board of directors. She then tried to change the subject by pointing to her work on health care while First Lady (*Huffington Post*, 2011)

"I hear you want to talk to me about your book."

Senator Clinton reaching out to author Steve Brill, who was working on a book about 9/11. Hillary and her staff tried to convince Brill it was she, and not Senator Schumer, who was responsible for helping many of the 9/11 families. However, Brill found out, "None of it turned out to be true . . . They gave me documents and phone calls and things like that which just plain never happened." (Newsmax.com, 2003)

"You don't understand. If we don't get this done this year, we are three years away from the benefits . . . So we've got to get it done right away, or we're going to be beaten in 1996."

First Lady Hillary about her healthcare reform plan (Woodward, *The Agenda*, 129). Liberal commentator Larry O'Donnell said of Hillary's plan, "It was extreme in its liberalism . . . it was the most liberal undertaking anyone had ever proposed. It was also utterly impossible . . . Zealotry was more the order of the day in the Clinton White House about health care." (*Frontline: The Choice '96*, PBS, 1996)

"I like it because I have an actual job to do, where what I'm doing is really the most important thing to the public."

Senator Clinton explaining why she likes being a US senator versus being just a first lady (USAToday.com, 2001). Chris Matthews said this of Hillary's political career, "Let's not forget—and I'll be brutal—the reason she's a U.S. senator, the reason she's a candidate for president, the reason she may be a front-runner is her husband messed around. That's how she got to be senator from New York. We keep forgetting it. She didn't win there on her merit. She won because everybody felt, 'My God, this woman stood up under humiliation,' right? That's what happened" (*Morning Joe*, 2008).

**VIDEO**

"Soon my staff became known around the White House as 'Hillaryland' . . . [They] prided themselves on discretion, loyalty and camaraderie, and we had our own special ethos."

Hillary explained in her book *Living History* (page 133). However, there was serious friction between the staffs of the first couple. "Bill Clinton staffers regarded the dwellers in Hillaryland as Kool-Aid drinkers with awful political judgment. Hillarylanders saw Bill's people as showboats and referred to them dismissively as the 'white boys.'" (*The New Republic Online*, 2006)

"Bill and I worked hard at our marriage with a great deal of mutual respect and deepening love for each other."

Hillary explained in her book *It Takes a Village* (page 43). Hamilton Jordan, chief of staff in the Carter Administration, wrote of the Clinton marriage: "[They] are not a couple but a business partnership, not based on love or even greed, but on shared ambitions. Everywhere they go, they leave a trail of disappointed, disillusioned friends and staff members to clean up after them. The Clintons' only loyalty is to their own ambitions." (*Wall Street Journal*, 2001)

"I had never before lived in a place so small, so friendly and southern, and I loved it."

Hillary expounding on her time in Arkansas in her book *Living History* (page 71). Hamilton Jordan also writes, "Arkansas was just a starting point for Bill Clinton and a place Hillary had to tolerate while nurturing national ambitions. It was their home for a quarter-century, the birthplace of their only child and their political base, but they left the state behind in favor of New York City, a place that can match the scale of their own egos, appetites and ambitions." (*Wall Street Journal*, 2001)

# BLAMING REPUBLICANS

"Taking such action for political purposes is simply reprehensible and should never be tolerated."

Hillary posted this statement about Lewis Libby's obstruction of justice indictment on her Senate Web page. Linda Tripp settled a lawsuit with the Department of Defense for $595,000 after the Clinton White House ordered contents of her personnel file to be leaked to try to damage her credibility in the early days of the Lewinsky scandal. The Clinton White House did this not because Ms. Tripp was lying but because she was telling the truth.

"I can tell you this: It's very hard to stop people who have no shame about what they're doing . . . It's very hard to stop people who have never been acquainted with the truth."

Senator Clinton in a speech to fellow Democrats, assailing Republicans (*New York Times*, 2005).

"[In] the 1980s, a lot of behavior that was counter-productive and antisocial took place in the board-rooms and highest political offices of America. It was an ethos that promoted 'every individual for himself,' a signal that permeated our life as a society."

Thanks to Bill and Hillary's leadership, there was no greed, or inappropriate behavior, in company boardrooms or oval office in the 1990s! (*Parade*, 1993)

"If New Yorkers can't trust him to keep his word for 10 days, how can they trust him for six years?"

Candidate Hillary Clinton lecturing her Senate opponent on the importance being honest with the voters (*New York Times*, 2000)

"I know a little bit about what it's like on the other end of Pennsylvania Avenue making these difficult decisions."

Hillary speaking to Tim Russert about her support of President Bush in the war on terror (*Meet The Press*, 2002).

However, just months later Hillary was criticizing Bush's decisions, "When the rest of the world opened its hearts to us [after 9/11] he turned his back and pursued a very narrow and unfortunate policy that we are still paying a very big price for" (*Newsmax*, 2003). Hillary neglected to mention that she voted to support President Bush's actions in Afghanistan and Iraq.

"I would say that there is a very well financed right-wing network of people that was after his Presidency from the very beginning. Really stopped at nothing, even to the point of perverting the Constitution in order to undermine what he was trying to do for the country."

Senator Clinton explained to Barbara Walters that she still believed the Republicans were to blame for the impeachment of her husband in the Monica Lewinsky matter (*Washington Times*, 2003). Even though it was revealed that Bill Clinton used a cigar on Monica's private parts and that he received oral sex from her after attending church on Easter Sunday, Hillary claims that the Republicans are the perverts from this scandal.

"Starr's distribution of his report was gratuitously graphic and degrading to the Presidency and the Constitution. Its public release was a low moment in American history."

In her book *Living History* (page 475), Hillary still blames Ken Starr, but not her husband, for degrading the presidency.

"If men like Starr and his allies could ignore the Constitution and abuse of power for ideological and malicious ends to topple a President, I feared for my county."

She also stated on page 472 of *Living History*. Ken Starr was never reprimanded or punished for his conduct in investigating the Clintons. The only person who was ever legally punished in the Lewinsky scandal was Bill Clinton, who was fined $90,000 by the judge in the case for making "intentionally false" answers in his deposition in the Paula Jones lawsuit. Clinton was also forced to surrender his law license, instead of being disbarred, for lying in the deposition.

"If we hadn't passed that big tax cut last spring, that I believe undermined our fiscal responsibility and our ability to deal with this new threat of terrorism, we wouldn't be in the fix we're in today."

Senator Clinton explaining that she believes that the Bush "tax cuts for the rich" are partially to blame for the 9/11 attacks and our inability to defeat the Taliban in Afghanistan. Just days later, the Taliban fled from Kabul and the town was liberated (CNN.com, 2001).

"But you know, you have got to hand it to them. These people are ruthless and they are relentless."

Just months after 9/11, Hillary addressed a crowd of Democrats and condemned the biggest enemy facing the country, the Republicans (*Newsweek*, 2002).

"I think that the stakes have been raised on the partisanship. There are so many people who shoot before they aim. They don't get the facts. They're quick to make outrageous statements and judgments about other people. . . . I don't think it's good for the country, that people scream at each other and accuse each other of things."

First Lady Hillary Clinton speaking out against the Republicans and all the unfair criticism she gets from them and the media (*Booknotes*, C-Span, 3/3/1996). Years later she would imply that "Bush Knew" about the 9/11 attacks in advance but did nothing to stop it.

**VIDEO**

"I predict to you that this administration will go down in history as one of the worst that has ever governed our country."

Senator Clinton speaking in Harlem where she apologized to a predominately black audience for the slow response to Hurricane Katrina by the Bush Administration (CNN.com, 2006). When you remember who she is married to, shouldn't she have used a different phrase other than, "go down in history"?

"When you look at the way the House of Representatives has been run, it has been run like a plantation, and you know what I'm talking about."

More from Senator Clinton's speech in Harlem, this time about the Republican-controlled House of Representatives.

**VIDEO**

"A tendency of this administration—from the top all the way to the bottom—is to withhold information . . . to refuse to be forthcoming . . . putting it all together, going back years now, there's a pattern and it's a pattern that should be troubling."

Senator Hillary Clinton criticizing the Bush administration and its culture of corruption in a press conference (*Washington Times*, 2006). Liberal pundit Joe Klein wrote of the Clintons' time in the White House and their inability to be truthful with the American people: "[With the Clintons] the story always is subject to further revision. The misstatements are always incremental. The 'misunderstandings' are always innocent—casual, irregular, promiscuous. Trust is squandered in dribs and drabs" (*Newsweek*, 1994). Klein wrote this four years before the world heard the name Monica Lewinsky.

"Our Constitution is being shredded. We know about the secret wiretaps, the secret military tribunals, the secret White House email accounts. . . . It's a stunning record of secrecy and corruption, of cronyism run amok."

Senator Hillary Clinton condemns the Bush White House practices on June 20, 2007.

VIDEO

"Well, I think a lot of people, frankly, have never really gotten to know me or had any direct contact with me."

Hillary's response when asked why she is disliked by so many rank-and-file Republicans (*Meet The Press*, 2004). It has nothing to do with her saying things like, "I've sometimes wondered that one cannot be a Republican and a Christian," does it?

"The consensus was the same, from the Clinton administration to the Bush administration . . . It was the same intelligence belief that our allies and friends around the world shared. . . . But I think that in the case of the [Bush] administration, they really believed it. They really thought they were right, but they didn't let enough sunlight into their thinking process to really have the kind of debate that needs to take place when a serious decision occurs like that."

Senator Hillary Clinton explaining her vote for the Iraq war, but then blaming Bush when no WMDs were found, because he actually believed what the CIA was telling him (*Larry King Live*, 2004). Years earlier, President Bill Clinton announced: "Earlier today, I ordered America's armed forces to strike military and security targets in Iraq. They are joined by British forces. Their mission is to attack Iraq's nuclear, chemical and biological weapons programs and its military capacity to threaten its neighbors . . . Saddam Hussein must not be allowed to threaten his neighbors or the world with nuclear arms, poison gas or biological weapons" (CNN.com, 1998).

"My husband did a great job in demonstrating that Democrats are not going to take these attacks. You know, all you have to do is read the 9/11 commission to know what he and his administration did to protect Americans, and to prevent terrorists attacks against our country."

Senator Clinton commenting on her husband losing his temper in an interview with Chris Wallace while appearing on the Fox News Network (MSNBC, 2006).

Michael Scheuer, who was the head of the CIA's Bin Laden unit during Clinton's presidency, said, "The former president seems to be able to deny facts with impunity. Bin Laden is alive today because Mr. Clinton, Mr. Sandy Berger, and Mr. Richard Clarke refused to kill him. That's the bottom line. And every time he says what he said to Chris Wallace on Fox, he defames the CIA especially, and the men and women who risk their lives to give his administration repeated chances to kill bin Laden." *(The Early Show, 2006)*

"I'm certain that if my husband and his national security team had been shown a classified report entitled 'Bin Laden Determined to Attack Inside the United States' he would have taken it more seriously than history suggests it was taken by our current president and his national security team."

Senator Clinton defending her husband's tirade while also criticizing the Bush administration, for failing to kill or capture Osama Bin Laden (CNN, 2006). Michael Scheuer rebutted this stating, "The fact of the matter is that the Bush Administration had one chance [to get Bin Laden] that they botched, and the Clinton Administration had eight to ten chances that they refused to try. At least at Tora Bora our forces were on the ground. . . . It's an incredible kind of situation for the American people over the weekend to hear their former president mislead them." (*The Early Show*, 2006) Scheuer went on to state, "Mr. Richard Clarke, Mr. Sandy Berger, President Clinton, are lying about the opportunities they had to kill Osama Bin Laden. That's the plain truth. That's the exact truth" (*Fox News Sunday*, 2006).

"Chelsea, we'll take a tour when someone decent lives there."

Circa 1985, Hillary's response when her young daughter asked to get a tour of the White House while the Clintons were in Washington to attend a function with President and Mrs. Reagan (Brown, *Crossfire*, 71). According to Brown, who was one of their Arkansas bodyguards, Hillary hated Republicans and Reagan in particular.

"The 1980s were about acquiring—acquiring wealth, power, privilege."

First Lady Hillary condemns "Reagan's Decade of Greed" (*Washington Post*, 1993). Hillary neglects to mention that in the 1980s she was a well-paid lawyer in a corporate law firm and sat on the board of directors of many companies, including Walmart.

"I believe in evil and I think that there are evil people in the world."

First Lady Hillary Clinton's opinion of the Washington establishment and those opposed to her plans to reform health care (Woodward, *The Agenda*, 169).

Hillary stated this just months after Islamic terrorists tried to kill tens of thousands of Americans in the World Trade Center bombing in 1993.

"I don't care how they do things around here. If they can't take the truth, at least they're going to get it from me."

First Lady Hillary talking about members of the Senate who had concerns about the high costs of her healthcare reform plan (Woodward, *The Agenda*, 169). J. Bradford Delong, who worked with Hillary on healthcare reform, once wrote, "My two cents worth, and I think it is the two cents worth of everybody who worked for the Clinton Administration on healthcare reform effort of 1993-1994, is that Hillary Rodham Clinton needs to be kept far away from the White House for the rest of her life. Heading up healthcare reform was the only major administrative job she has ever tried to do. And she was a complete flop at it . . . [She] has already flopped as a senior administration official in the executive branch—the equivalent of an Undersecretary. Perhaps she will make a good senator. But there is no reason to think that she would be anything but an abysmal president" (*National Review*, 2003).

"What are you doing inviting these people into my home? These people are our enemies. They are trying to destroy us."

First Lady Hillary fuming to an aide when she found out the aide invited some Republican senators and congressmen to the Clinton White House (Harris, *The Survivor*, 99). Hillary made this statement about her enemies just months after the World Trade Center bombing of 1993.

"They can't really take me on, on the issues . . . so they practice what I call the politics of personal destruction."

Senator Clinton, always criticizing Republicans, while on her book tour of *Living History* (AP, 2003).

"Vice President Cheney came up to see the Republicans yesterday. You can always tell when the Republicans are getting restless, because the Vice President's motorcade pulls into the Capitol, and Darth Vader emerges."

Senator Clinton at a Democratic fundraiser (CNN, 2007)

"They're more interested in tax cuts for the rich than for flu shots for everyone who needs them."

Senator Clinton blaming the Bush Administration tax cuts for the supposed flu vaccine shortage in 2004 (AP, 2004).

"This is national crisis and a flat-out moral failing."

Senator Clinton criticizing Bush Administration policies (letter from Hillary posted at HillaryClinton.com, 2006).

Hillary has never stated that what her husband did with Monica was a moral failing.

"I have been absolutely amazed, even shocked, at the combination of arrogance and incompetence that marks this particular administration."

Senator Clinton speaking to Jane Pauley (SFGate.com, 2006)
     She was speaking of the Bush Administration, not the future administration.

**VIDEO**

"You know, absolute power not only corrupts, but it can lead to bad decisions."

Senator Clinton criticizing the Bush Administration (Press release of Senator Clinton, 9/6/2006). Hillary's husband once said in anger, "I'm president of the United States. I can do any goddamned thing I want. I take care of my friends and fuck my enemies" (*Capitol Hill Blue*, 1999).

**VIDEO**

"[Republicans] want to keep power for the sake of power, and they want to be sure that nothing upsets their plans to be able to pursue their own agendas . . . undermining public education, undermining health care availability, undermining Social Security."

First Lady Hillary speaking just prior to the 1998 midterm election, while her husband was embroiled in the Monica Lewinsky scandal (*Online Newshour*, 1998).

"Americans have the right to expect discipline and responsibility from their leaders, and we have some suggestions for how to do that."

Senator Clinton criticizing the Bush Administration (DLC.org, 7/24/2006).

The administration Hillary later worked for ended up having a few issues regarding discipline, honesty, and responsibility themselves. What does she think of IRS targeting, Benghazi, HealthCare.gov rollout, Fast & Furious, Bowe Bergdahl prisoner swap, Snowden affair, Solyndra, Veterans Affairs, mass surveillance of US citizens, hacking of AP & Fox News journalists, etc?

VIDEO

# HILLARY ON WATERGATE

"I had been on the impeachment staff back in 1974 and I had actually researched the historical and legal grounds for impeachment. And I knew that what was being attempted against [President Clinton] was absolutely out of line with what the founders had thought, what people had always believed was the basis for Constitutional impeachment."

Senator Hillary Clinton speaking on her book tour promoting *Living History* (*Larry King Live*, 2003). The man who supervised then-twenty-seven-year-old Hillary Rodham during Watergate, Jerry Zeifman—a lifelong Democrat—says that she "engaged in a variety of self-serving, unethical practices in violation of House rules." Because of the behavior he witnessed, he also states, "Hillary Clinton is ethically unfit to be either a senator or president." When asked why, he states, "Because she was a liar." Contrary to Internet rumors, Zeifman did not fire her from the committee, saying, "If I had the power to fire her, I would have fired her." Why? "Because of her unethical conduct" (*The Neal Boortz Show, 2008*).

"I've always said I thought Richard Nixon absolutely made the right decision for the country by resigning and sparing the country a trial in the Senate and all the anguish that would have produced."

Years before the impeachment of Bill Clinton, First Lady Hillary gave her opinion of Nixon's decision to resign before being impeached (Radcliffe, *Hillary Rodham Clinton: A First Lady For Our Time*, 256).

The late Barbara Olson wrote of Hillary's corruption: "It is more than a little ironic that Hillary was a staffer on the House Judiciary Committee that prepared articles of impeachment against President Richard Nixon, because she's very much like the public's image of Nixon: ambitious, cold, ruthless, and willing to evade, stonewall, or even lie when it serves her purpose." (Olson, *The Final Days*, 13)

# I'M NOT RUNNING FOR OFFICE, TAKE MY WORD

"People have said that to me, but it is something I don't take seriously at all; it's not even in the universe of thinking."

First Lady Hillary's response when asked if she'd ever run for president. (*60 Minutes II*, 1999)

"People think that because I care so much about public issues, I should run for office myself. I don't want to run for office."

Clinton's seems definitive on page 63 in the book she wrote with Osborne, *The Unique Voice of Hillary Rodham Clinton.*

"Not that I can imagine. No, that is anything I have ever thought of for myself. I must say I really admire people like my husband, who are willing to face the heat of politics, especially today."

Her response when asked if she'd ever consider running for political office at some future point. (*Larry King Live*, 1997)

**ARTICLE**

"I have said that I'm not running and I'm having a great time being pres—being a first-term senator . . . [Y]ou guys are going to get me in a lot of trouble."

Senator Clinton in a speech at The National Press Club. (AP, 2001)

"You know Tim, I have no intention of running for president."

Hillary to journalist Tim Russert. (*Meet The Press*, 2001)

**VIDEO**

"I have no plans to run for president."

Another denial to Tim Russert (*Meet The Press*, 2002). It was discovered she seriously considered running in 2004, even setting up an operation, but decided against it after deciding to fulfill her pledge of serving her full six-year term. (Heilemann and Halperin, *Game Change*, 20)

"I have absolutely no interest in running for president again."

A pledge of Secretary of State Hillary Clinton after she lost the 2008 primary contest to Barack Obama. (ABCNews.com, 2009)

# "Hello, Iowa. I'm baaaaack! . . . It's true: I am thinking about it."

Hillary Clinton at the Harkin Steak Fry, September 15, 2014. It was her first trip to Iowa since the 2008 Iowa Caucuses.

Biographers Heilemann and Halperin captured Hillary's true feelings of the Hawkeye State. "If Hillary was going to be competitive in Iowa, she would need to go all out. The problem was, she hated it there. . . . She found Iowans diffident and presumptuous; she felt they were making her grovel. . . . She bitched about Iowa's scruffy hotels and looked for excuses to avoid staying overnight." (Heilemann and Halperin, *Game Change*, 94)

**VIDEO**

## RESULTS OF THE 2008 DEMOCRATIC PRIMARY

Barack Obama: 38%

John Edwards: 30%

Hillary Clinton: 29%

"Politics is so unpredictable; whoever runs has to recognize that the American political system is probably the most difficult, even brutal, in the world."

Hillary told Jane Pauley when she asked Hillary—practically begged her—to enter the 2016 presidential race. (CNS News, 2014)

Hillary thinks it's so brutal because it lasts so long? Ms. Pauley, who campaigned for Barack Obama in 2008, sounds as if she'll volunteer on Hillary's campaign in 2016. How brutal that Hillary must put up with these difficult questions!

"I think you're being very persistent, but you are playing with my words and playing with what is such an important issue. . . . I think you're trying to say that I used to be opposed, and now I'm in favor, and I did it for political reasons, and that's just flat wrong."

Hillary Clinton getting testy with NPR's Terry Gross over Hillary's changing position on same-sex marriage. (*Fresh Air*, 2014)

In January 2000 Hillary said that marriage does not include gay unions: "Marriage has got historic, religious and moral content that goes back to the beginning of time, and I think a marriage is as a marriage has always been: between a man and a woman." In 2013 her position had changed to, "I support marriage for lesbian and gay couples. I support it personally and as a matter of policy and law embedded in a broader effort to advance equality and opportunity for LGBT Americans and for all Americans." (*Washington Post*, 2013)

VIDEO

# WORKS CITED

Alfano, Sean. "Osama's Health Still A Mystery." CBS News, September 25, 2006. Accessed February 14, 2015, http://www.cbsnews.com/news/osamas-health-still-a-mystery/.

Allen, Mike. "Obama turns tables on Clinton." Politico, February 20, 2008. Accessed February 12, 2015, http://www.politico.com/news/stories/0208/8594.html.

"America's New War." CNN.com. November 10, 2001. Accessed February 13, 2015, http://transcripts.cnn.com/TRANSCRIPTS/0111/10/se.03.html

Bacon, Perry Jr. "Hillary Clinton Returns to Iowa for Senator Tom Harkin." NBC News, September 14, 2014. Accessed February 10, 2105, http://www.nbcnews.com/politics/hillary-clinton/hillary-clinton-returns-iowa-senator-tom-harkin-n203336.

Bernstein, Carl. *A Woman In Charge*. New York: Knopf, 2007, 552, 554

Birnbaum, Gregg. "Polygraph: Hill Accuser Honest – He Passes Test Jewish Slur." New York Post, August 22, 2000. Accessed February 9, 2015, http://nypost.com/2000/08/22/polygraph-hill-accuser-honest-he-passes-test-jewish-slur/

Brock, David. *The Real Anita Hill: The Untold Story*. New York: Touchstone, 1994.

Brock, David. *The Seduction of Hillary Rodham*. New York: Free Press, 1996.

Brown, L. D. *Crossfire: Witness in the Clinton Investigation*. Ld Brown, 1999.

Bruck, Connie. "Hillary the Pol." New Yorker, May 30, 1994. Accessed February 9, 2015, http://www.newyorker.com/magazine/1994/05/30/hillary-the-pol.

Buchanan, Bay. *Extreme Makeover of Hillary (Rodham) Clinton*. Washington, DC: Regnery, 2007.

Bunch, Will. "Exclusive: Clinton acknowledges a "misstatement" on Bosnia sniper fire." Attytood Blog, Philly.com, March 25, 2008. Accessed February 12, 2015, http://www.philly.com/philly/blogs/attytood/Exclusive_Clinton_acknowledges_a_misstatement_on_Bosnia_sniper_fire.html.

Burry, Chris. Interview with George Stephanopoulos. Frontline, 2000. Accessed February 11, 2015, http://www.pbs.org/wgbh/pages/frontline/shows/clinton/interviews/stephanopoulos.html

"Button gaffe embarrasses Clinton." BBC News, March 7, 2009. Accessed Februry 11, 2015, http://news.bbc.co.uk/2/hi/7930047.stm.

Califano Jr, Joseph A. *Inside: A Public and Private Life*. New York: PublicAffairs, 2005.

"CBS News Video Contradicts Clinton's Story." CBS News, March 24, 2008. Accessed February 12, 2015, http://www.cbsnews.com/news/cbs-news-video-contradicts-clintons-story/.

Chait, Jonathan. "In Gaffe, Hillary Clinton Endorses Communism." New York Magazine, October 27, 2014. Accessed February 11, 2015, http://nymag.com/daily/intelligencer/2014/10/gaffe-hillary-clinton-endorses-communism.html.

Chapman, Stephen. "Hillary On Health Care: The Perils Of Arrogance." Chicago Tribune, May 30, 1993. Accessed February 11, 2015, http://articles.chicagotribune.com/1993-05-30/news/9305300079_1_health-insurance-system-of-medical-care-mrs-clinton.

Clinton, Hillary. "'Baby fat' is no laughing matter." Post Star, July 19, 2005. Accessed February 12, 2015, http://poststar.com/opinion/commentary/baby-fat-is-no-laughing-matter/article_bd783d20-2f48-59e8-bf40-95d0acef4409.html.

Clinton, Hillary Rodham. *Hard Choices*. New York: Simon & Schuster, 2014.

Clinton, Hillary Rodham. Interviewed on *Larry King Live*, June 10, 2003.

Clinton, Hillary Rodham. *It Takes A Village: And Other Lessons Children Teach Us*. New York: Simon & Schuster, 1996.

Clinton, Hillary. *Living History*. New York: Scribner, 2004.

Clinton, Hillary Rodham and Claire G. Osborne. *The Unique Voice of Hillary Rodham Clinton: A Portrait in Her Own Words*. New York: Avon Books, 1997.

"Clinton's 'plantation' remark draws fire." CNN.com. January 18, 2006. Accessed February 13, 2015. http://www.cnn.com/2006/POLITICS/01/17/clinton.plantation/.

"Clinton: Rich 'Not Paying Their Fair Share' in Taxes." Fox News, May 28, 2010. Accessed February 11, 2015, http://www.foxnews.com/politics/2010/05/28/clinton-rich-paying-fair-share-taxes/.

Clinton, William J. "The President's News Conference." January 9, 1996. Accessed February 10, 2015. Online by Gerhard Peters and John T. Woolley, The American Presidency Project. http://www.presidency.ucsb.edu/ws/?pid=52570.

Davis, Lanny. "Why I am ready for Hillary." The Hill, December 10, 2014. Accessed February 9, 2015, http://thehill.com/opinion/lanny-davis/226723-lanny-davis-why-i-am-ready-for-hillary.

"Democrats accuse Cheney, Bush of 'troubling' secrecy." Washington Times. February 14, 2006. Accessed February 14, 2015, http://www.washingtontimes.com/news/2006/feb/14/20060214-111130-1008r/

Donaldson, Sam. "Hillary Clinton and The Other Woman." ABC's *Prime Time Live*, January 30, 1992. Accessed February 7, 2015, http://vimeo.com/111902721.

Dowd, Maureen. "Obama's Big Screen Test." *New York Times* Opinion, February 21, 2007. Accessed February 9, 2015. http://www.nytimes.com/2007/02/21/opinion/21dowd.html.

Eisenberg, Rebecca. "First lady just doesn't get it." SF GateFebruary 22, 1998. Accessed February 12, 2015, http://www.sfgate.com/business/article/First-lady-just-doesn-t-get-it-3103744.php.

Fineman, Howard. "The First Families Square Off." October 28, 2002. Accessed February 13, 2015. http://www.freerepublic.com/focus/news/777541/posts.

Fouhy, Beth. Clinton feels heat over Wal-Mart ties." AP News, March 10, 2006. Reported in Boston Globe, March 12, 2006. Accessed March 2, 2015, http://www.boston.com/news/nation/articles/2006/03/12/clinton_feels_heat_over_wal_mart_ties/.

*Frontline: The Choice '96.* PBS, 1996. Accessed February 13, 2015, http://www.pbs.org/wgbh/pages/frontline/shows/choice/.

Gergen, David. *Eyewitness To Power: The Essence of Leadership Nixon to Clinton.* New York: Simon & Schuster, 2001.

Gerth, JEFF and DON VAN NATTA Jr. "Hillary's War." New York Times Magazine, May 29, 2007. Accessed February 12, 2015, http://www.nytimes.com/2007/05/29/magazine/03Hillary-t.html?pagewanted=all.

Goldberg, Jeffrey. "Hillary Clinton: 'Failure' to Help Syrian Rebels Led to the Rise of ISIS." The Atlantic, August 10, 2014. Accessed February 11, 2015, http://www.theatlantic.com/international/archive/2014/08/hillary-clinton-failure-to-help-syrian-rebels-led-to-the-rise-of-isis/375832/.

Guarino, David R. "Hill at Tufts: Use Bible to guide poverty policy." *The Boston Herald*, November 11, 2004.

Hakim, Danny. "Hillary, Not as in the Mount Everest Guy." *New York Times*, October 17, 2006. Accessed February 11, 2015, http://www.nytimes.com/2006/10/17/nyregion/17hillary.html.

Halper, Daniel. *Clinton, Inc.: The Audacious Rebuilding of a Political Machine.* New York: Broadside Books, 2014.

Harris, John. *The Survivor: Bill Clinton in the White House.* New York: Random House, 2006.

Harnden, Toby. "Nobel winner: Hillary Clinton's 'silly' Irish peace claims." Daily Telegraph, March 8, 2008. Accessed March 2, 2015, http://www.telegraph.co.uk/news/worldnews/1581150/Nobel-winner-Hillary-Clintons-silly-Irish-peace-claims.html

Haster, Dennis. Speaker: Lessons from Forty Years in Coaching and Politics. New York: Regnery, 2004.

Healy, Patrick, D. "Senator Clinton Assails Bush and G.O.P. at Campaign Fund-Raiser." New York Times, June 6, 2005. Accessed February 9, 2015, http://www.nytimes.com/2005/06/06/nyregion/06cnd-hillary.html?pagewanted=print&_r=1&.

Heilemann, John and Mark Halperin. *Game Change: Obama and the Clintons, McCain and Palin, and the Race of a Lifetime.* New York: Harper Perennial, 2010.

Heinhold, Florian. "A Heated Exchange for Hillary." ABC News, April 14, 2007. Accessed February 12, 2015, http://abcnews.go.com/blogs/politics/2007/04/heated_meeting_/.

Helderman, Rosalind S., and Philip Rucker. "Plans for UCLA visit give rare glimpse into Hillary Clinton's paid speaking career." Washington Post, November 26, 2014. Accessed February 11, 2015, http://www.washingtonpost.com/politics/plans-for-ucla-visit-give-rare-glimpse-into-hillary-clintons-paid-speaking-career/2014/11/26/071eb0cc-7593-11e4-bd1b-03009bd3e984_story.html.

"Hillary Clinton Aide Tells Reporter To 'Fuck Off' And 'Have A Good Life.'" BuzzFeed, September 24, 2012. Accessed February 12, 2015, http://www.buzzfeed.com/buzzfeedpolitics/hillary-clinton-aide-tells-reporter-to-fuck-off#.xiaWMVWZx.

"Hillary goes conservative on immigration." Washington Times, December 13, 2004. Accessed February 12, 2015, http://www.washingtontimes.com/news/2004/dec/13/20041213-124920-6151r/?page=all.

"Hillary Speaks: Part II." 60 Minutes, May 26, 1999. Accessed February 9, 2015, http://www.cbsnews.com/news/hillary-speaks-part-ii/.

"Hillary to Iowans: I Comforted Troops at Walter Reed." *Newsmax.* November 16, 2003. Accessed February 13, 2015, http://www.freerepublic.com/focus/f-news/1022674/posts

Hubbell, Web. *Friends In High Places: Our Journey from Little Rock to Washington, DC.* New York: William & Morrow & Co., 1997.

Hughes, Brittany M. "Hillary: 'American Political System is Probably Most Difficult, Even Brutal, in World'" CNS News, June 16, 2014. Accessed February 10, 2015, http://www.cnsnews.com/news/article/brittany-m-hughes/hillary-american-political-system-probably-most-difficult-even-brutal.

Humbert, Marc. "Clinton Makes a Pitch for Women." AP Blog, August 30, 2006. Accessed February 12, 2015, http://www.foxnews.com/printer_friendly_wires/2006Aug30/0,4675,NATNYPOLITICSWeblog,00.html.

Hume, Brit. "Former Head of CIA bin Laden Unit Says Clinton Had 10 Chances to Get Terror Mastermind. Fox News Sunday, September 26, 2006. Accessed February 14, 2015, http://www.foxnews.com/story/2006/10/01/transcript-counterterror-experts-debate-clinton-claims-on-fns..

Isikof, Michael. "First Whitewater prosecutor says 'serious crimes' were uncovered in probe." *Yahoo News*, October 7, 2014. Accessed February 13, 2015, http://news.yahoo.com/first-whitewater-prosecutor-says--serious-crimes--were-uncovered-in-probe-220111087.html.

Johnston, David Cay. "SPENDING IT; It Takes a President To Overpay the I.R.S." New York Times, April 19, 1998. Accessed February 9, 2015, http://www.nytimes.com/1998/04/19/business/spending-it-it-takes-a-president-to-overpay-the-irs.html.

Jonas, Michael. "Sen. Clinton urges use of faith-based initiatives." *Boston Globe*, January 20, 2005. Accessed February 8, 2015, http://www.boston.com/news/local/massachusetts/articles/2005/01/20/sen_clinton_urges_use_of_faith_based_initiatives/.

Jordan, Hamilton. "The First Grifters." Wall Street Journal, February 19, 2001. Accessed February 12, 2015, http://www.wsj.com/articles/SB982638239880514586.

Kelly, Michael. "Saint Hillary." *New York Times Magazine*, May 23, 1993.

Kessler, Ronald. *First Family Detail.* New York: Crown Forum, 2014.

Kessler, Ronald. *A Matter of Character: Inside the White House of George W. Bush.* New York: Sentinel, 2004.

Kessler, Ronald. *The Secrets of the FBI.* New York: Crown Forum, 2012.

Khan, Huma. "Hillary Clinton: 'Absolutely No Interest' in Another Presidential Run; 'No' to Running for Governor or Senate Again, Too." ABC News, October 14, 2009. Accessed February 10, 2015, http://abcnews.go.com/blogs/politics/2009/10/hillary-clinton-absolutely-no-interest-in-another-presidential-run-no-to-running-for-governor-or-sen/.

Kiely, Kathy. *USA Today.* July 10, 2001. Accessed February 13, 2015, http://usatoday30.
usatoday.com/news/washington/july01/2001-07-10-hillary.htm.

Kiely, Kathy and Jill Lawrence. "Clinton makes case for wide appeal." USA Today, May
8, 2008. Accessed February 12, 2015, http://usatoday30.usatoday.com/news/politics/
election2008/2008-05-07-clintoninterview_N.htm.

Klein, Edward. *Blood Feud: The Clintons vs. The Obamas.* Washington DC: Regnery, 2014.

Klein, Edward. *The Truth About Hillary.* New York: Sentinel, 2005, 184-185.

Klein, Joe. "The Politics Of Promiscuity." Newsweek, May 8, 1994. Accessed February 14,
2015, http://www.newsweek.com/politics-promiscuity-188618

Koppel, Ted and Jackie Judd. "Making Hillary Clinton An Issue." Frontline, March 26,
1992. Accessed February 12, 2015, http://www.pbs.org/wgbh/pages/frontline/shows/
clinton/etc/03261992.html.

Letter from Hillary Clinton on fixing health care. Posted at Free Rebublic, January 23, 2006.
Accessed February 14, 2015, http://www.freerepublic.com/focus/f-news/1563417/posts.

Limbacher, Carl. *Hillary's Scheme.* New York: Crown Forum, 2003.

Lizza, Ryan. The New Republic Online. February 20, 2006. Accessed February 13, 2015,
http://www.newrepublic.com/article/guide-the-clinton-juggernaut.

MacMinn, Aleene. "Pop/rock." *Los Angeles Times* Morning Report, January 29, 1992.
Accessed February 7, 2015, http://articles.latimes.com/1992-01-29/entertainment/
ca-767_1_singer-tammy-wynette.

Meet the Press, NBC September 15, 2002. Accessed February 13 2015, https://cps.nbclearn.
com/html/nbcarchive/cuecards/4136.html.

Milton, Joyce. *The First Partner: Hillary Rodham Clinton.* New York: Harper, 2000.

"Mogul Pays Off No. 3, Weds No. 4." New York Post, July 22, 2000. Accessed February 9,
2015. http://pagesix.com/2000/07/22/mogul-pays-off-no-3-weds-no-4/?_ga=1.24781
1335.1462527672.1422723362.

Morris, Dick. *Rewriting History.* New York: Harper, 2005.

MSNBC, November 22, 2014. Accessed February 12, 2015, http://www.msnbc.com/msnbc/
hillary-clinton-obama-immigration-order-historic-step.

Nagourney, Adam. *New York Times.* October 9, 2000. Accessed February 13, 2015, http://
www.nytimes.com/2000/10/09/nyregion/campaign-2000-new-york-politely-lazio-mrs-
clinton-debate-un-supreme-court.html

"New CBS Video Contradicts Clinton Again." CBS News, March 25, 2008. Accessed February
12, 2015, http://www.cbsnews.com/news/new-cbs-video-contradicts-clinton-again/.

Noonan, Peggy. *The Case Against Hillary Clinton.* New York: Harper, 2000.

Olson, Barbara. The Final Days. Washington, DC: Regnery, 2003.

"Once Upon A Time in Arkansas." *Frontline,* 1997. Accessed February 13, 2015, http://www.
pbs.org/wgbh/pages/frontline/shows/arkansas/etc/synopsis.html

Oppenheimer, Jerry. *The State of A Union.* HarperCollins, 2000.

Patterson, Buzz. *Dereliction of Duty: Eyewitness Account of How Bill Clinton Compromised
America's National Security.* Washington, D.C: Regnery, 2004.

Pilkington, Ed. "Hillary Clinton interview: will she or won't she run for president in 2016?" Guardian, June 21, 2014. Accessed February 11, 2015, http://www.theguardian.com/world/2014/jun/22/-sp-hillary-clinton-interview-will-she-run-for-president-2016.

Purdum, Todd S. "Hillary Clinton Meets Man Who Gave Her 2 L's." *New York Times*, April 3, 1995. Accessed February 11, 2015, http://www.nytimes.com/1995/04/03/world/hillary-clinton-meets-man-who-gave-her-2-l-s.html

Rabinowitz, Dorothy. "Juanita Broaddrick Meets the Press." *Wall Street Journal*, February 19, 1999. Accessed March 2, 2015, http://www.wsj.com/articles/SB919379691540145000.

Radcliffe, Donnie. Hillary Rodham Clinton: A First Lady for Our Time. New York: Grand Central Publishing, 1993.

Rogin, Josh. "Exclusive: 'Hillary Clinton Took Me Through Hell,' Rape Victim Says." The Daily Beast, June 20, 2014. Accessed February 12, 2015, http://www.thedailybeast.com/articles/2014/06/20/exclusive-hillary-clinton-took-me-through-hell-rape-victim-says.html.

Schweizer, Peter. *Do As I Say (Not As I Do): Profiles in Liberal Hypocrisy*. New York: Anchor, 2006.

Seitz-Wald, Alex. "In NYC, Hillary Clinton calls Obama's immigration action 'historic'

"Senator Clinton Gets Pulled Into Presidential Pardon Scandal." *Crossfire*, February 22, 2001. Accessed February 12, 2015, http://www.cnn.com/TRANSCRIPTS/0102/22/cf.00.html.

"Senator Reasserts Right-Wing Conspiracy." June 9, 2003. Accessed February 13, 2015. http://www.washingtontimes.com/news/2003/jun/9/20030609-122659-8346r/?page=all

"She apologized for not giving a tip." Washington Times, February 16, 2000. Accessed February 11, 2015, http://www.washingtontimes.com/news/2000/feb/16/20000216-010909-5235r/.

Sheehy, Gail. Hillary's Choice. New York: Ballantine Books, August 15, 2000.

Sheehy, Gail. "What Hillary Wants." *Vanity Fair*, May 1992. Accessed February 7, 2015, http://www.vanityfair.com/news/1992/05/hillary-clinton-first-lady-presidency.

"Steven Brill: Hillary Fabricated 9/11 Records." *Newsmax*. April 20, 2003. Accessed February 13, 2015, http://www.freerepublic.com/focus/f-news/896912/posts

Stewart, James. *Blood Sport: The Truth Behind the Scandals in the Clinton White House.* New York: Simon & Schuster, 2012.

Suarez, Fernando. "Clinton Says She and McCain Offer Experience, Obama Offers Speeches." CBS News, March 1, 2008. Accessed February 12, 2015, http://www.cbsnews.com/news/clinton-says-she-and-mccain-offer-experience-obama-offers-speeches/.

Tasini, Jonathan, *Huffington Post*, May 25, 2011. Accessed February 13, 215, http://www.huffingtonpost.com/jonathan-tasini/hillary-and-walmart-a-lov_b_15235.html

Van Auken, Bill. "Iraq war is the real underlying crime' in the Libby indictment." World Socialist Web Site. October 29, 2005. Accessed February 13, 2015, http://www.wsws.org/en/articles/2005/10/libb-o29.html.

"We Are All Responsible," Parade, April 11, 1993, http://news.google.com/newspapers?nid=13 50&dat=19930411&id=Y0xPAAAAIBAJ&sjid=TAMEAAAAIBAJ&pg=4586,3192439.

Weiner, Rachel. "How Hillary Clinton evolved on gay marriage." Washington Post, March 18 2013. Accessed February 10, 2015, http://www.washingtonpost.com/blogs/the-fix/wp/2013/03/18/how-hillary-clinton-evolved-on-gay-marriage/.

Wills, Christopher. "Obama's thin, but varied record." USA Today, January 16, 2008. Accessed March 2, 2015, http://usatoday30.usatoday.com/news/politics/2008-01-16-2414012588_x.htm.

Woodward, Bob. *The Agenda: Inside the Clinton Whitehouse*. New York: Simon & Schuster, 2005.

Woodward, Bob. *Shadow: Five Presidents and the Legacy of Watergate*. New York: Simon & Schuster, 2000.

Zeleny, Jeff and Julie Bosman. "Obama Rejects Idea of Back Seat on Ticket." New York Times, March 11, 2008. Accessed February 12, 2015, http://www.nytimes.com/2008/03/11/us/politics/11clinton.html?pagewanted=all&_r=0.

Zeleny, Jeff. "Working Together, Obama and Clinton Try to Show Unity." New York Times, June 28, 2008. Accessed February 12, 2015, http://www.nytimes.com/2008/06/28/us/politics/28unity.html?pagewanted=print&gwh=38857DA5D2AD992F225A43D07C110C6F&gwt=pay.

# ACKNOWLEDGMENTS

Many thanks to Geoff Stone, Kelsey Whited, and everyone else at WND Books.

Also thanks to Bobby Gee, Lisa Bloom, and Mariah Wills for all of your help and dedication to this publication.

Thanks to my lovely wife, Denise, for all of her support. And most of all, special thanks to Hillary Rodham Clinton for supplying all of the material used in this book.

# ABOUT THE AUTHOR

Tom Kuiper grew up in Sibley, Iowa, and graduated from Iowa State University with a degree in Communications. He's worked on projects for the conservative website Newsmax.com and was the researcher behind the popular Deck of Hillary playing cards, one of the site's most successful products ever. He lives in his hometown and works as a paralegal for a major corporation.

CPSIA information can be obtained at www.ICGtesting.com
Printed in the USA
LVOW04s2250290415

436556LV00005B/5/P